A WORKBOOK

The Water Age

Art and Writing Workshops

Tracey Warr

MEANDA BOOKS

Meanda Books
https://meandabooks.com

Cover by James A. Hudson

Book Layout © 2017 BookDesignTemplates.com

The Water Age #2: Art and Writing Workshops/ Tracey Warr. -- 1st ed.
ISBN 978-0-9954902-3-9

The Water Age Series

The Water Age and Other Fictions (#1)
The Water Age Art and Writing Workshops (#2)
The Water Age Children's Art and Writing Workshops (#3)

The Water Age is a series of three books by Tracey Warr. The books contemplate water and futures through fiction and through art and writing workshops. The books were produced as part of the *Frontiers in Retreat* project. They were co-produced by HIAP, with the support of the EU Culture Programme.

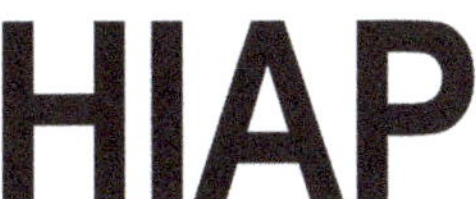 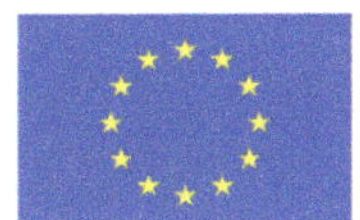

This project has been funded with support from the European Commission. This publication reflects the views only of the author, and the Commission cannot be held responsible for any use which may be made of the information contained therein.

CONTENTS

{ 1 }

Topic—The Water Age

The art and writing workshops in this book engage creatively and playfully with the possibility that we may be living with more water in the future. The workshops were all devised and presented by me over the course of a number of art projects which are detailed in the Thanks section of this book. By collecting the workshops together in this book, I hope that other artists, writers and workshop leaders will be able to adapt and use them and generate more stories and images relating to the endlessly fascinating topic of water.

Rivers and oceans cover 70% of the planet and are part of an interconnected system with atmosphere, weather and ice caps. Gravitational pulls between the Earth and the Moon affect the ebbs and flows of water. A small change in one place can have significant ramifications far away and elsewhere. In this cycle, water is evaporating from the ocean, travelling through the air, raining down on the land and flowing back to the ocean. There is constant flux and sometimes dramatic change: storm surges, hurricanes, tsunami, floods. The majority of scientists agree that water levels are rising, and will continue to do so for centuries, due to the thermal expansion of the oceans and melting ice sheets. The Intergovernmental Panel on Climate Change (IPCC) estimates that there will be between a 7" and a 2' rise in water levels by 2099 (Intergovernmental Panel on Climate Change). Other researchers have claimed that the IPCC's figures are conservative and estimate instead between a 2' and 6' [2m] rise. The Netherlands are planning for a 4' rise by 2100 and a 13' [4m] rise by 2200. In the extreme scenario that all the ice caps melt, predictive flood maps show the UK as an archipelago with many major cities under water (Predictive flood maps).

Rising water levels will create climate refugees. Around 634 million people live in coastal areas. Low-lying countries and islands including the Maldives, Tuvalu and Bangladesh and the east coast of the United States will be amongst the most affected areas.

Changing temperatures and water levels have always happened. There have been at least five Ice Ages and the Little Ice Age in the 16th to 19th centuries, and now we are heading into what we might call The Water Age.

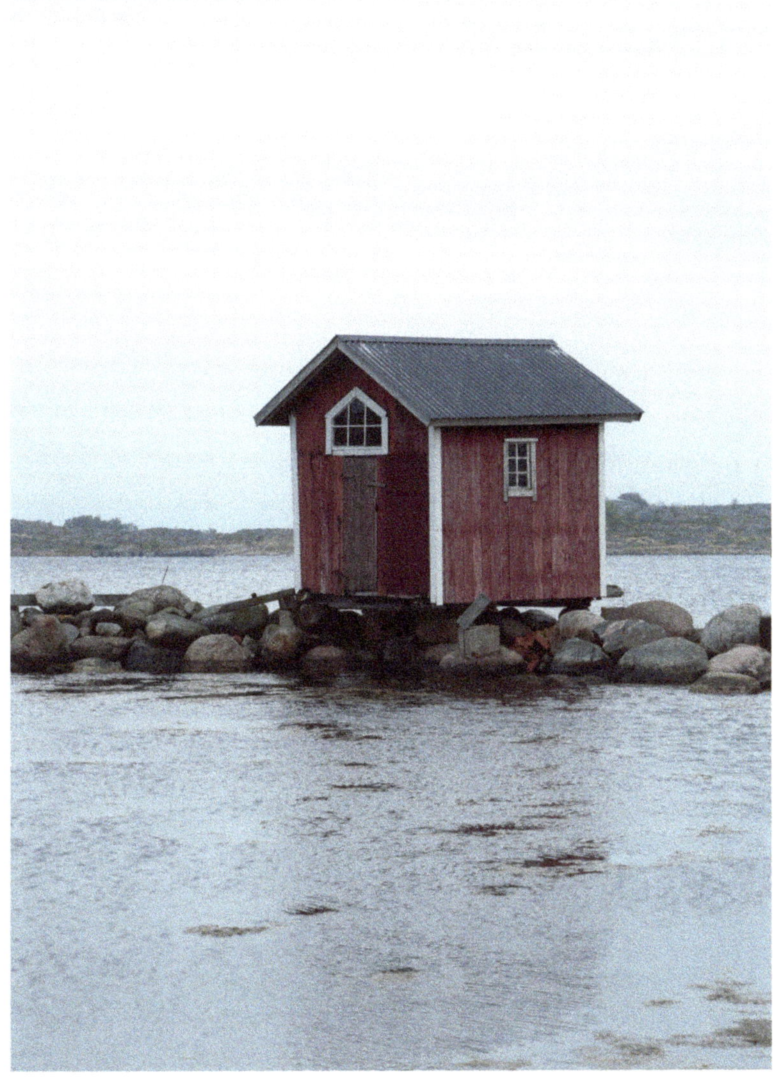

Utö Island, Turku Archipelago, Finland. *Frontiers in Retreat* Incubator event, 2015. Photo by Bruce Gilchrist.

We have already experienced extreme flooding all around the world in the last few years. And we can see that rising water levels are not just about coastal areas, because of the interconnected nature of the whole system. Rivers are affected along their entire lengths; the water table and subterranean water levels are affected. Eventually these waters recede but, eventually, some of them will not.

How might we react to rising water levels? Coastal retreat is one option but migration on that scale would significantly impact on population densities inland. There might be a further role for sea and flood defences and water management, but given the scale of the problem, the element of futility, the enormous cost and our current economic crises—that may not be the solution.

Instead of a dystopic disaster scenario we could try to imagine solutions and adaptations. It is well-established that science fiction has influenced technological developments (European Space Agency, 2009). Artists can propose what appear to be unfeasible solutions that nevertheless inspire future development. We could imagine living happily with more water, going with the flow and thinking about the potential beneficial impacts on our values and how we live. Cnut, the 11th century Danish king of England, sat on the beach on a throne commanding the sea to stay back, in order to demonstrate to fawning courtiers his impotence in the face of the incoming tide. This is an interesting story if we consider that the

Vikings were perhaps the closest humans have come to being amphibian.

We may have evolved from aquatic ancestors. Syndactyly—webbed toes or fingers—is a recognised condition that occurs in around 1 in every 2,500 people. Many people feel hydrophilia—a love of being in water, and water can induce a dream-like state of mind.

Will our bodies evolve to cope with an aqueous world? In the meantime, can we imagine other ways of living with liquid? We could study aquatic mammals, plants, birds, insects and fish to inspire us. Biomimicry looks at natural forms but also at the amazing functions and technologies that animals and plants have evolved to survive in their environments.

A few examples of biomimicry are: camouflage inspired by natural surroundings (desert, woodland, jungle) and by creatures that camouflage themselves to blend in, Velcro inspired by the burdock burr, swimsuits based on shark skin, fibre optic cable inspired by sea sponges, the Shinkansen bullet train influenced by kingfishers, tape imitating gecko suckers, wind turbine design influenced by hump back whales, sensors imitating rats' whiskers (Benyus, 1997). Many areas of technology, robotics and architecture draw on biomimicry (Pawlyn, 2011). Underwater search vehicles are based on fish, earthquake search robots are based on snakes that can wiggle through rubble, mimicking dolphin sounds has enhanced long distance underwater transmissions. Vincent Callebaut's floating climate refugee cities are based on lilypads (Callebaut). Ron Herron suggested cities that could be raised on robotic legs to wade through water (Herron).

{ 2 }

Aquatic Biomimicry

Place white paper tablecloths on tables and tape them down with masking tape so that they do not slip around.

Discuss with others seated at your table how you might live in the future Water Age.

Decide on one or more things that you would like to envisage for daily life to cope with this increased aquatic environment. It might help to think of *Star Trek,* in which the future is pictured through a simple set of imagined technologies, but you should also apply biomimetic principles, based on aquatic flora and fauna, to your inventions. Find out about how various forms of aquatic life adapt and thrive in watery environments.

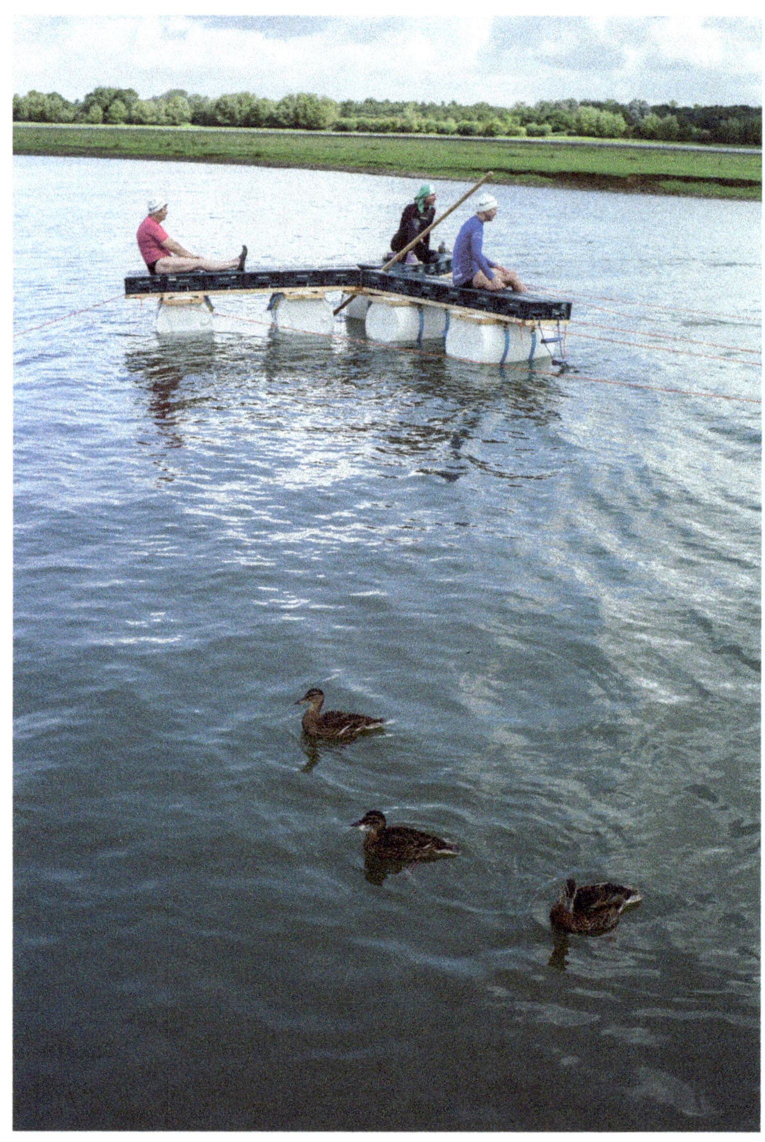

The Wet Symposium, River Thames, Oxford, 2012.
Photo by James A. Hudson.

What daily technologies might we need for amphibian conditions: clothing, housing, food and drinking water, warmth, mobility, recreation.

What happens to art, books or cats?

How do we keep things dry that have to be dry?

Can we sleep in water?

Can we learn from the acoustic underwater communication of aquatic lifeforms?

Draw or write your imagined inventions on your table cloths.

Collect relevant materials. Translate your ideas into models.

Set up a test tank—a bowl or large fish tank full of water. Test out your models.

{ 3 }

Walking, Mapping, Writing

Bring maps that include waterscapes—rivers, coastal areas, lakes. Discuss the significance of maps for writing.

You may find Peter Turchi's book *Maps of the Imagination: The Writer as Cartographer* (2007) very helpful for this workshop.

Write Maps

Look at the words that relate to water on the map and on the map legend.

Compile a selection of those words.

Write a prose-poem with those words.

Write a flash fiction (very short) including those words, imagining your way into the map.

Take a Line for a Walk

Wear walking shoes.

Plot a short walk (maximum one hour) alongside a nearby river on a map. Select four stopping points on the map.

Walk along the river. Consider how the river has shaped the landscape around it. Consider its relationship with flora and fauna that you encounter. Attend to what you can see, but also to sounds, smells and textures. Imagine what might be beneath the ground. Look up to the sky.

Stop at the four points you selected on the map and write down a sentence.

Collect a portable object on the walk.

Writing

Returning to your base room, study your four sentences. Develop them into a short piece of writing.

Contemplate the object you picked up. What does it look like, feel like, smell like? Imagine its history and its future. Imagine what is going on inside it. Write a short piece from the point of view of your object.

Present your writings on a local radio station.

{ 4 }

Viking Readings of the Marine Environment

As landlubbers, most of us tend to view the sea from the perspective of the land. What if you could turn this inside out? What if your perspective were that of a seabird or a fish or a Viking seafarer? How does a sea-based perspective change your observations?

For Viking communities, the seas and waterways were a means of transportation and contact, rather than barriers. In an age when the magnetic compass was unknown, Viking explorers went all over Europe and Russia, and discovered Iceland, Greenland and Newfoundland. During the Middle Ages, most seafaring relied on coastal navigation—steering from one known landmark to the next. Viking ships, on the other hand, plied directly across the ocean between Norway and Greenland, making direct crossings of the North

Sea and wide stretches of the Atlantic. They used close observation of their environment to navigate, employed the accounts of other Viking sailors who had gone before them, and developed early navigation instruments.

Viking directions from Norway to Greenland, for example, read:

> *From Hernar in Norway one should keep sailing west to reach Hvarf in Greenland and then you are sailing north of Shetland, so that it can only be seen if visibility is very good; but south of the Faeroes, so that the sea appears half-way up their mountain slopes; but not so far south of Iceland that one only becomes aware of birds and whales from it. (Sawyer, 2001, p. 198)*

Even when land was below the horizon, certain signs showed its direction: cloud formations, the reflected light which icefields cast into the sky, the presence of seabirds and their lines of flight. Vikings used bird augury, for example, setting free ravens—Odin's birds—and observing their flightpaths, but there was also a practicality in that. Hungry birds, flying high, will head for land that sailors at sea-level cannot yet see.

On long ocean crossings, far out of reach of any land, Viking seafarers used latitude sailing, as in the instructions for Greenland above. Storms, however, might drive a ship off course. Then they would have to locate themselves using sun and stars. Latitude could

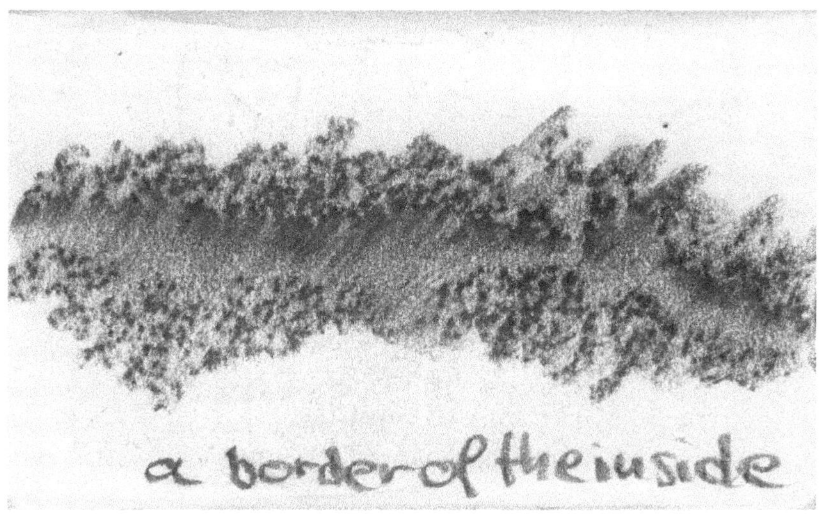

Kati Gausmann, A border of the inside, rock rubbing from Utö Island, Turku Archipelago, Finland. Frontiers in Retreat Incubator event, 2015, from the series dancing dough and other circumstances. Courtesy of the artist. Photo by Salla Lahtinen.

be calculated using the sun's maximum height at noon. If the sun stood higher in the sky than before, they were too far south; if lower, they were too far north. A man named Star Oddi, living in Iceland in the 12th century, made a set of tables giving the sun's midday height for every week of the year.

A person holding at arm's length a stick marked off in units could record the sun's height and estimate latitude by comparison with that of other places known to them. The shadow cast at noon could be measured.

It is easier to make calculations using the Pole Star, but in northern latitudes during the summer months, the night sky is too bright for stars to be visible. An Icelander on pilgrimage to Jordan in the 12th century lay flat on his back, raised one knee, placed his fist on his knee with the thumb pointing upwards. The Pole Star appeared exactly at the tip of his thumb (Sawyer, 2001).

In fog or cloud, Viking seafarers had to wait for better visibility and then recalculate their course. But they also used a piece of Iceland spar, known as sunstone, to scan the sky in cloudy conditions. The sunstone polarised light.

They used a bearing dial with reference to the sun or Pole Star to guide their steering, which might have a shadow pin and a moveable pointer to mark the course. Old Norse has eight points of the compass: North, South, East, West, Landnorth (NE), Landsouth (SE), Outnorth (NW), Outsouth (SW). A 12th century bearing dial found in Greenland had 32 compass points. To take a bearing, the navigator would turn it till the notch representing the south pointed to the spot where a vertical line drawn from the midday sun would cut the horizon—this would then give all the other points of the compass and the course could be altered accordingly. At night, a bearing could be taken aligning the northern notch with the Pole Star if it was visible.

From experience, a Viking seaman would know at what precise point the sun would rise at the season of his journey and then bearings could be taken at dawn, rather than waiting for midday. Star Oddi also composed seasonal sunrise tables.

Observation/Notation Exercises

Go on a ferry or other boat. Make your own close observations of the environment you are passing through: land, clouds, birds, driftwood, sun, the shape of waves, the colour of water.

Try writing your own version of directions for the sea journey you are taking (like the directions from Norway to Greenland, above).

Try using your body as a measuring/navigating instrument, like the Icelandic pilgrim to Jordan. Work in pairs or small groups if you like.

Maps and sea charts have been developed to represent journeys. Invent your own system for noting your observations on a blank sea chart of the area you are moving through.

{ 5 }

Writing with Water

Read Tristan Gooley's *How to Read Water* (2017) in advance of this workshop.

Go on a ferry or other boat journey and note down words that occur to you as you look at the water environment around you. From these words, tease out some thematics that you are interested in.

The aim in this workshop is simple—to create actions, texts and images relating to water. But, of course, that is not really simple, because water is such a vast and varied subject. We could think about rising coastal levels and flooding predicted to occur as a result of climate change, or we might consider biological, astronomical, geological, metaphorical, psychological (and many other) aspects of water.

The significances of water are ambiguous. Its vastness might be construed as sublime. Its unseen depths might be experienced as fearful. Alongside its positive aspects, it may be associated for some people with dissolution and death. Water is a vast topic. Identify your focus, your raft, within this vastness. Use a large sheet of paper to diagram possibilities for your focus.

With your focus in mind, explore an island or a coastal area or another type of waterscape (river, brook, lake).

You can work in twos, threes, or individually.

Try out some of the following exercises that appeal to you and invent your own.

Document your exercises using phone cameras or recorders, drawings or written notes.

Suggested Exercises

Give yourself a focus/constraint for your observations such as doors, marine objects, a particular colour or sound, edges, curves and lines.

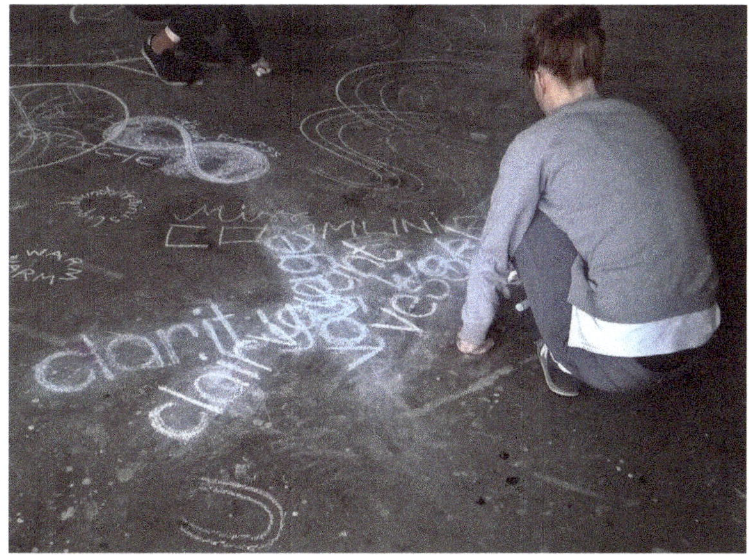

Writing with Water Workshop led by Tracey Warr, HIAP, Suomenlinna Island, 2016. Part of *Frontiers in Retreat*. Photo by Tracey Warr.

Use your body as a measure.

Follow water.

Write a short text or individual words in blue or green chalk on the ground. In choosing a site think about the relationship between site and text.

Write a word in water with a calligraphy brush.

Reflect the world in a bowl(s) of water.

Use a water-filled jar as a magnifying glass.

Produce your own hydramap of your locale.

Photograph places and objects that show the traces of water.

Create actions/movements that explore the water in your body in relation to the water in the environment.

Find a place where you can see water, that seems significant to you (significance might be political, sensory, metaphorical, biological, geological, irrational etc.). Sit there for five minutes looking. Write some notes. Close your eyes. Sit there for five minutes listening, smelling, touching. Write some notes. Stand up. Close your eyes. Move around (a little or as much as you feel confident, without falling in any water!). Write some notes. Review your notes, underlining words and phrases that seem key to you. Write a short text.

Create drawings relating to your findings on water.

Study things upside-down, reflected in water.

Draw a map of the line you intend to travel. Stop at frequent intervals to either write, make an image (drawing or photo), make a documented action/movement or sketch a plan for an action.

Make sound recordings on your phone of water sounds. If you have waterproof equipment or hydrophones you could record underwater sounds.

And you will have many more ideas….

Bring your documentations of exercises back, present and discuss with each other.

{ 6 }

Ecology of Words

A two-day workshop (or longer). (This workshop was originally designed to take place on an island. You can adapt it to your local waterscape.)

Pretask Instructions

Prior to the workshop, select three words related to water and send them to the workshop leader. They can be words in English or another language. They will be words you might like to take on an adventure during the workshop. You will not be pinned down to 'your' three words and may end up working with other words.

The workshop leader should collate these words, print them out on sticky labels, stick them on small boxes to be arranged in a pile

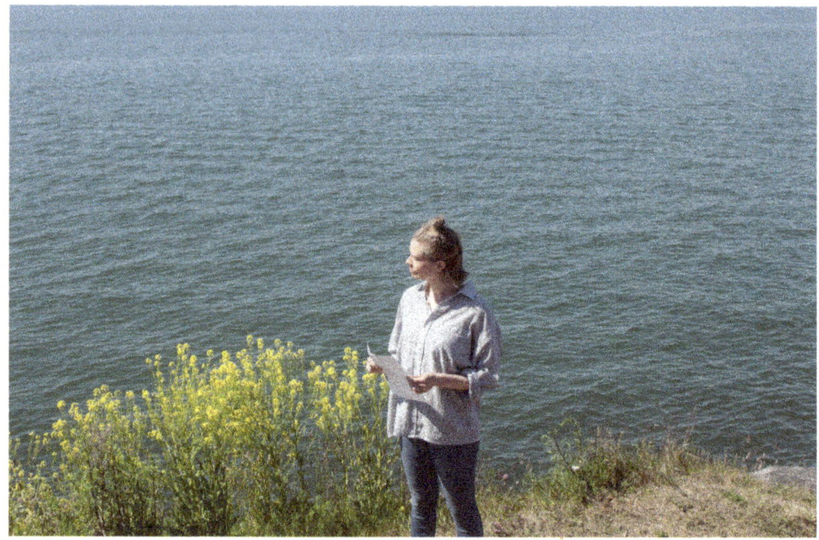

Ecology of Words Workshop led by Tracey Warr, HIAP, Suomenlinna Island, Helsinki, Finland, 2017. Part of *Frontiers in Retreat.* Photo by Salla Lahtinen.

in the workspace. Reference images and short texts can be put on the wall. The methods below could be printed out and stuck onto cards for ease of use.

Materials: a blackboard, chalk, a floor you can chalk on (it can be easily mopped off with water), four small handheld flags, maps of the small area you are working in. If possible (via institutional library access), provide online access to the full *Oxford English Dictionary* in the workspace.

DAY ONE

Workshop Introduction

Language is often accused of being a mechanism of power—and certainly language has been and is used to control, dominate, colonise, hierarchise, suppress. In her book, *Unmarked*, published in 1993, Peggy Phelan pointed out that language is often binary—black/white, male/female—with one side of the binary assumed to be the norm that the counterpart is othered against to its detriment.

Of course, there is some truth to the thesis that language is oppressive power play but, in this workshop, I would like to concentrate on some more positive aspects of language. I am a writer, so I am not interested in merely critiquing anthropocentric logocentrism. Words and text are my material and I think of myself as working with them as a sculptor works with stone, wood or bronze. Words and language are our best approximation at articulating our own experience to ourselves and attempting to share that with other humans.

The meaning of words are often contested. Words can be slippery. What do we each mean when we use the words nature or ecology, for examples. Most words have at least two meanings and many words have considerably more than two meanings, as James Joyce demonstrated in *Finnegans Wake*. There may be some words in our vocabulary that we are convinced we know the meaning of but our use of them is, in fact, eccentric. Despite dictionary definitions and a constant pressure for consensus about language and its meaning, language can be just as subjective in its meaning as colour, taste or smell. The comprehension of words between us is not precise.

We might think of words as labels for boxes that we put tangled complexes of meaning into. We then manipulate these word-box-labels between us to approximate shared understanding—but rather than the exchange of words between one conscious person and another being like a definite lock of understanding, nebulous understandings slide between us with the words; comprehension smears rather than clicks into place.

And if you extend that inaccurate slide of language to the non-human then the potential for disunderstanding is of course exponentially greater. This disunderstanding applies to the human-machine interface as well as to the human-animal interface. Algorithms are constantly attempting to read and interpret us. The languages of nonhuman others include the pulsing of stars, the rhythms of tides, birdsong, dogs barking, the kinaesthesia of plants and trees. How might we put de-defining and misunderstanding to use in our various art, writing and life practices?

As well as being controlling, language can also be expansive, creating, conjuring, fluid. It is alive in the sense that we are making it up and making it mean in our mouths and on the page all of the time.

Are there words that do not exist yet that you need to express something? Are there words we need to make mean differently? Have you come across any coinages, newly minted words, in your reading or writing in relation to ecology?

Are there ways for us to make our deployment of language more expressive, articulate and inventive? The writer, George Eliot, said that her life's ambition was to write beautiful sentences. Are there ways that our use of language might help us move past an impasse in our thinking and acting?

Since language is living and fluid and contested, definitions always have to be at least discursive. This workshop takes an even more radical approach to language, seeking to extend, invent and undo definitions. We are going to materialise words, putting them into poetic play, stretching them from the inside. We are going to help words bloom.

On the first day, we are going to largely play with individual words, using our base and its vicinity to take them on adventures. Tomorrow we will think more about where that gets us and what we want to do with language in our own practices. Tomorrow you might want to create your own personal dictionary, or spill a story or account from one word, or install a text somewhere, or voice or perform your findings. Tomorrow you will think about stringing together words or spilling them out of these boxes. We will think about whether it is possible to be anti-taxonomic. But today we should just do, and play with the material of words. And there should not be too much rationale to play.

Of course, working with the nuances, associations, histories and potentials of words is a richer experience if you are working in your own language rather than a second or third language. If you want to work in your own language, please do. You may need to then share your findings in the shared language of the workshop.

Or, you may choose to work in English (or another language), even if it is not your first language. Something very interesting also happens in non-native use of a language.

Three key starting points for this workshop were Robert Smithson's artwork *Heap of Language* (1970), Lewis Carroll's nonsense poem, 'Jabberwocky', and Georges Bataille's non-definition of *l'informe* or formless in 'The Critical Dictionary'.

> *'Twas brillig, and the slithy toves*
> *Did gyre and gimble in the wabe;*
> *All mimsy were the borogoves,*
> *And the mome raths outgrabe. (Carroll, 2015)*

> **FORMLESS**.-*A dictionary begins when it no longer gives the meaning of words, but their tasks. Thus, formless is not only an adjective having a given meaning, but a term that serves to bring things down in the world, generally requiring that each thing have its form. What it designates has no rights in any sense, and gets itself squashed everywhere, like a spider or an earthworm. In fact, for academic men to be happy, the universe would have to take shape. All of philosophy has no other goal: it is a matter of giving a frock coat to what is, a mathematical frock coat. On the other hand, affirming that the universe resembles nothing and is only formless amounts to saying that the universe is something like a spider or spit. (Bataille, 1985)*

Bataille's point is that it is not what words mean, but what they do/perform/enact that we should focus on. Bataille considered that rational thought was unable to cast even a dim light on the problems of life that he wished to explore. When he hit limits in his system he would resort to images, poetic invective or fiction, which is the role of the earthworm, the spider and the spit in his definition of formless. Many of 'The Critical Dictionary' entries were tracing leakages and pollutions across the binary divide.

There are many other creative dictionaries preceding and following Bataille's. Flaubert was working on a *Dictionary of Received Ideas*. Bataille's friend Michel Leiris compiled his own personal dictionary. The Surrealists Paul Eluard and Andre Breton compiled a *Dictionnaire Abrege du Surrealism*. These initiatives were aiming to subvert the exclusive and definitive quality of dictionaries, to find new meanings inside words. They searched for 'words still unknown, and burning to be uttered', for 'future words and expressions'.

Perhaps binaries should not be discarded. We could think of binaries pulsing, meanings pulsing back and forth, as the tides go in and out, we breath in and out, the heart beats on and off, as stars pulse.

1. WORDS. Consider the pile of words. You are not obliged to work with 'your own' words. You can add a few words to this heap if you have a burning desire to do so. Make a list of words you would like to play with in your notebook. How many is up to you. It could be 1 or 10 or however many of these words are calling out to you. You may find as the day goes on that you need to add more to your initial selection or subtract some. Eventually you will be working with a more or less stable group of words over the two days.

2. POST. 'Self-document' and distribute the workshop with tweets or Instagram or Facebook posts on the hour throughout the workshop. Make it a quick sentence or two, or a photo. Use whichever mode of posting you want and chop and change if you like. Use your own accounts to post but always include a consistent hashtag such as #ecologyofwords.

If you prefer not to engage with social media, devise another way of hourly self-documenting such as writing a sentence on the floor, sticking a sentence on the wall, leaving a message somewhere for a stranger to find.

3. METHODS. Look through the pile of methods below. Add methods to the pile. Select a few that appeal to you and make a note in your notebook.

4. PARTNER. Choose a partner to work in dialogue with for some initial actions in the morning. Change partner after lunch and again after tea. Come back to briefly share your first adventures before lunch and do not forget to post or tweet on the hour. Continue with these actions in the afternoon, so that you cover a number of words and actions.

Methods

box

Feel free to use the other faces of some of the boxes to add translations in various languages you know. Put synonyms and antonyms, etymologies and other information or items you find relevant to the word inside the box. Add your own invented definitions. Rearrange the boxes if you feel like it. Keep rearranging them.

dictionary

Check your word in the *Oxford English Dictionary*. Consider how you might expand and adapt its definitions, synonyms and antonyms. Undefine it. Using free association, add unexpected definitions or small objects to the word box.

blackboard/diagram

Use a blackboard to create a diagram relating to the definitions and/or uses of your word. You can also chalk on the floor to create a diagram.

coining

What word do you need that doesn't exist yet—to describe a concept or a knot of ideas? Or just to be a more effective adjective, adverb, noun for a particular use? Shakespeare coined words. Bataille's 'l'informe' is a coined word. Theorists often coin words to reach at new concepts, for example, Donna Haraway's 'Chthulucene'. Russell Hoban's novel of a post-nuclear world, *Riddley Walker*, is written in an invented/adapted language. See Lewis Carroll's explanations for his nonsense words in 'Jabberwocky' (Gardner, 2000). Invent a word and write out definitions for it in dictionary-style.

prefix

Try adding non, un, de, sub, anti, etc. if your word doesn't usually take those, and invent new definitions.

topography typography

Take your word on an adventure outside, matching word to to-pography appropriately or inappropriately. Where does your word want to be sited? Mould your word into a grassy hollow. Write it on a beach, or with stones or other found materials. Kick it down a hill, etc.

eavesdrop

Find a fairly crowded place where you can sit still. Listen to word usage by passing people. Make some notes. You might record references to your word, associations with your word, redefinitions for your word that you can derive from overheard phrases, or some other word may emerge from what you hear.

usepath

Architect Sarah Wigglesworth, often uses motion trace drawings to design living and working spaces. Could the movements of words be traced on the ground? On a map? As a drawing? Starting at the exit from the gallery look for signs of your word and follow its usepath or desire line around the island (or the area that you are working in). Draw its usepath on the map or otherwise create a usepath drawing for your word.

name

Take a blank map of the island and walk around naming places and areas.

label

Use your word as an appropriate or inappropriate label. Photograph it in situ.

unidentified objects

Look for objects in the landscape with no obvious clear use. Name them. Invent uses/definitions for them.

unknown

In his poem, 'Difference', Mark Doty writes:

What can words do

but link what we know

to what we don't,

and so form a shape? (Doty, 1995)

Find something unknown in the area you are exploring. Try and explain the inexplicable by linking it through words to what is known.

formless

Look for spiderwebs, spit, worms, slime trails, shadows, bird tracks, wrack line, birdshit, lichen, flight of birds or planes across the sky, movement of water around submerged rocks etc., and interpret these as messages. Take photos. What other words might be worth listing if the universe is something like a spider or spit?

liquid words

Float words in various liquids, in bowls, puddles, lakes and out to sea. (Tip: pencil persists best in water.) Put words in wine glasses with water and play the glasses. Wash words.

semaphore

Look up Flag Semaphore online. Stand some distance apart with a view of each other with two flags each. Using Semaphore, one of you should send your selected word to the other. The other should reply with a word coming from free association. Continue.

morse code

Look up Morse Code online. Using a mirror, sunlight and Morse Code, one of you should send your selected word to the other. The other should reply with a word coming from free association. Continue.

see through

Write antonyms of your word in steam on windows and mirrors or write on tracing paper and view from the other side.

corner a word

If you drive a word into a corner, capture it between things or other words, does it give you a new or clearer meaning?

converge

Converge your word with other words in chalk on the floor or on the blackboard. (See the illustration on page 23.)

notations

Contemplate the use of crosshatching, scoring through, bracketing or of notation languages such as dance writing, proofreading symbols or short-hand.

biffuring

Take a short text. Erase particular words.

horizon

Sit somewhere and write the line of the horizon using words or one repeated word.

wearable

Find ways to wear your word and strut, glide etc., it around the island or your area as appropriate or inappropriate.

dance

Develop a dance for your words. Plot out the dance with footsteps in chalk on the floor for others to follow.

sing

Sing your word to the sea or the sky or a tree or a rock or a passing stranger.

trace

Look for traces of your word in the vicinity.

ken

A kenning is a circumlocution, an ambiguous or roundabout figure of speech used instead of an ordinary noun in Old Norse, Old English and later Icelandic poetry. A few examples:

life-liquid	blood
bane of wood	fire
lip-streams	poetry
whale-road	sea
sea-steed	ship
sky-candle	sun
breaker of trees	wind

Invent kennings for your word and put them in the word box. Invent kennings for things observed around you.

hum

Hum your word in a variety of places. Set it into resonance and vibration.

collective nouns

Examples of watery collective nouns include a gulp of cormorants, a bask of crocodiles, a pod of dolphins, a paddling of ducks, a bed of eels, a school of fish, a flamboyance of flamingos, a bloat of hippopotamuses, a smack of jellyfish, a convent of penguins, a lamentation of swans. Invent a new collective noun for something watery that you observe.

taking a line for a walk

'A drawing is simply a line going for a walk.' 'A line is a dot that went for a walk.' Paul Klee

Go for a walk with your word, drawing your walk onto a blank map and stopping at four spots which you should mark on the map. At each of those four spots use your word in a sentence. String together your four sentences.

constraints

Constrained writing is a literary technique where certain things are forbidden, or certain patterns are imposed. The Oulipo group, including Georges Perec, are amongst famous exponents of constrained writing methods. Try out one or more of the following techniques:

> Univocalic poetry, using only one vowel.
>
> Mandated vocabulary, where the writer must include specific words.
>
> Alliteratives or tautograms, in which every word must start with the same letter (or subset of letters).
>
> Lipogram: a letter (commonly e or o) is outlawed.

Abecedarius: first letter of each word/verse/section goes through the alphabet.

Palindromes, such as the word 'radar', read the same forwards and backwards.

Anglish, favouring Anglo-Saxon words over Greek and Roman/Latin words.

Limitations in punctuation, such as no commas.

Or you can use length constraints, e.g.:

Six-Word Memoirs: 6 words

Haiku: ~ 3 lines (5–7–5 syllables or 2–3–2 beats recommended.)

Minisaga: 50 words, +15 for title

Drabble: 100 words

Twiction: microfiction where a story or poem is exactly 140 characters long.

conflate

Conflate your word with another word. For example, in the preface to *The Hunting of the Snark*, Lewis Carroll describes the following procedure to develop 'those frumious jaws':

Take the two words 'fuming' and 'furious'. Make up your mind that you will say both words, but leave it unsettled which you will say first. Now open your mouth and speak. If your thoughts incline ever so little towards 'fuming', you will say 'fuming-furious'; if they turn, by even a hair's breadth, towards 'furious', you will say 'furious-

fuming'; but if you have that rarest of gifts, a perfectly balanced mind, you will say 'fruminous'. (Gardner, 2000)

portmanteau

Develop your word into a series of portmanteau words. A portmanteau word is a word packed, like a suitcase, with more than one meaning. The great master of the portmanteau word is James Joyce, especially in *Finnegans Wake*. Some contemporary examples: agit-prop, bionics, brunch, chexting, chocoholic, cyborg, ecocide, emoticon, facsicle, ginormous, guestimate, humungous, labradoodle, mocumentary, pictionary, prequel, quark, serendiculous, zillionaire.

spill

A long roll of paper with thoughts spills from one initial word written on it and the scroll rolls down a steep hill, cladding the topography. What can you spill from a word?

field recordings, the language of others

Make field recordings of water.

archaeology of words

Select a watery site. What words can you collect from that site?

embodied writing

Use parts of your body as writing instruments: foot, elbow, mouth, etc.

repeat

Repeat your words as a chant or incantation.

sayings

List sayings you are aware of. For examples:

It's raining like a pissing cow.

The time between the dog and the wolf (= twilight).

He is horny like a hot rabbit.

A rolling stone gathers no moss.

A bird in the hand is worth two in the bush.

Too many cooks in the kitchen spoil the broth.

Invent some new ones.

Devil's dictionary

Bierce's *Devil's Dictionary* included entries such as:

Egotist (n.) A person of low taste, more interested in himself than in me.

Lawyer (n.) One skilled in circumvention of the law.

Start inventing your own dictionary.

DAY TWO

Actions

Discuss any overnight thoughts about yesterday's exercises. Choose to do one of the following today:

Create your own dictionary
Spill a story or an account from one word
Install a text inside or out
Perform or voice a text.

Spend the morning planning and developing, and then the afternoon presenting and having a wrapping up discussion. Continue with your hourly posts.

Do not feel too precious or anxious about what you do. Whatever it is, it is quick; it is provisional. It can take any form—an image or text you print out or write out and put on the wall, a voicing, a performance, some footage or sound that you show through your phone or a laptop, something you chalk on the pristine blackboard or the floor. You can use an interior or an exterior space. You can collaborate or work individually.

You will have 5–10 minutes each to present. Spend an hour preparing, thinking and then start. Put together a schedule in some logical order, especially if some of you are taking the group out and about.

Give each other comments on each presentation.

Hold a final, rounding up conversation after tea.

Resources for Further Study

Some of the following books and websites may be useful.

Bachelard, Gaston (1983) *Water and Dreams*, Dallas: Pegasus Foundation and Dallas Institute of Humanities and Culture.

Ballard, J.G. (2014) *The Drowned World*, London: Fourth Estate.

Bataille, Georges (1985). *Visions of Excess: Selected Writings 1927-1939*, (A. Stoekl with C.R. Lovitt & D.M. Leslie Jr. Trans.). Manchester: Manchester University Press.

Benyus, Janine M. (1997) *Biomimicry: Innovation Inspired by Nature*, New York: Morrow.

Callebaut, Vincent vincent.callebaut.org

Carroll, Lewis (2015) *The Complete Alice: Alice's Adventures in Wonderland and Through the Looking-Glass and What Alice Found There*, London: Macmillan.

Cheever, John (1990) *Collected Stories*, London: Vintage.

Deakin, Roger (2000) *Waterlog: A Swimmer's Journey Through Britain*, London: Vintage.

Doty, Mark (1995) 'Difference'. *Poetry Foundation.* www.poetryfoundation.org/poems/44136/difference-56d2231d9f249

European Space Agency (2009) *Innovative Technologies from Science Fiction* www.esa.int/esapub/br/br176/br176.pdf

Fishman, Charles (2011) *The Big Thirst: The Secret Life and Turbulent Future of Water,* New York: Free Press.

Gardner, Martin, ed. (2000) *The Annotated Alice*, New York: W.W. Norton.

Gilchrist, Bruce; Joelson, Jo & Warr, Tracey, eds. (2015) *Remote Performances in Nature and Architecture*, London: Routledge.

Gooley, Tristan (2017) *How to Read Water: Clues & Patterns from Puddles to the Sea*, London: Sceptre.

Frontiers in Retreat www.frontiersinretreat.org

Herron, Ron, *Walking City on the Ocean* www.moma.org/collection/works/814

Intergovernmental Panel on Climate Change www.ipcc.ch

Macfarlane, Robert (2007) *The Wild Places*, London: Penguin.

Pawlyn, Michael (2011) *Biomimicry in Architecture*, London: RIBA Publishing.

Pollack, Sydney/Perry, Frank (1968) *The Swimmer*, film.

Predictive Flood Maps flood.firetree.net

Remote Performances www.remoteperformances.co.uk

Robinson, Kim Stanley (2004) *Forty Signs of Rain*, New York: Harper Collins.

Sawyer, Peter (2001) *The Oxford Illustrated History of the Vikings*, Oxford: Oxford University Press.

Turchi, Peter (2007) *Maps of the Imagination: The Writer as Cartographer*, San Antonio, Texas: Trinity University Press.

Warr, Tracey (2018) *The Water Age and Other Fictions*, London: Meanda Books.

The Wet Symposium/River Runs vilma.cc/river.

Thanks

I undertook research on the overall topic for these workshops as part of the *Frontiers in Retreat* project during residencies with Jutempus in Lithuania, HIAP in Finland and Centre d'Art i Natura in Catalonia/Spain, and on a fieldtrip to Utö Island. Many thanks to Nomeda and Gediminas Urbonas (Jutempus), Jenni Nurmenniemi, Jaana Eskola, Salla Lahtinen and all the staff at HIAP, and Lluís Llobet, Cesca Gelabert and Arnau Llobet and the inhabitants of Farrera.

Several of these workshops were first presented as part of *Frontiers in Retreat*. I am indebted to all the members of the *Frontiers in Retreat* network, and especially to those artists who were in residence alongside me: Tuula Närhinen, Quelic Berga, Anna Rubio, Hanna Husberg, Elena Mazzi, mirko nikolic and Kati Gausmann.

This book is based on a series of workshops that I devised and led, which are detailed below. Sources on the art projects mentioned can be found in the Resources for Further Study section of this book. An immense thank you to all the participants in these workshops whose inspiring contributions spurred me to put together this book, hoping that other groups might use the exercises.

The Aquatic Biomimicry Workshop was first devised for OVADA in Oxford in 2012. Many thanks to OVADA, and especially to Adrian Pawley.

Many thanks to Tim Eastop at the Canal & River Trust, to Russell Robson at the Environment Agency, and Oxford Brookes University for their support of *The Wet Symposium* in the River Thames and the *River Runs* project at Modern Art Oxford in 2012. And thanks to my collaborators in *River Runs*: Nomeda and Gediminas Urbonas, and Giacomo Castagnola. Laura Degenhardt did a terrific job as Project Assistant. Thanks to those who joined us for the Learning from the River Workshop at MIT, which I led with Gediminas Urbonas, and for *Future Rivers* in Oxford.

The Walking, Mapping, Writing Workshop was first presented for the *Remote Performances* project organised in 2014 by London Fieldworks at *Outlandia,* with radio broadcasts in collaboration with Resonance 104.4fm. Thanks to Bruce Gilchrist and Jo Joelson and the other artists in the project. Many thanks to the Lochaber

Highlands Archive and Glen Nevis Visitor Centre who hosted that first workshop.

The Viking Readings of the Marine Environment Workshop was presented for *Frontiers in Retreat* on the ferry to Utö Island in 2015.

The Writing with Water Workshop was presented for *Frontiers in Retreat* at HIAP on Suomenlinna Island, Helsinki, Finland in 2016. Thank you to Kira O'Reilly and students from the MA in Ecology and Contemporary Performance at University of the Arts, Helsinki.

The Ecology of Words Workshop was presented for Frontiers in Retreat at HIAP on Suomenlinna Island, Helsinki, Finland in 2017.

Thanks to Bruce Gilchrist, James A. Hudson, Kati Gausmann, Salla Lahtinen and Sergio Urbina for permission to use their photographs. And, finally, I am extremely grateful to James A. Hudson for his beautiful work on the book covers for The Water Age series.

ABOUT THE AUTHOR

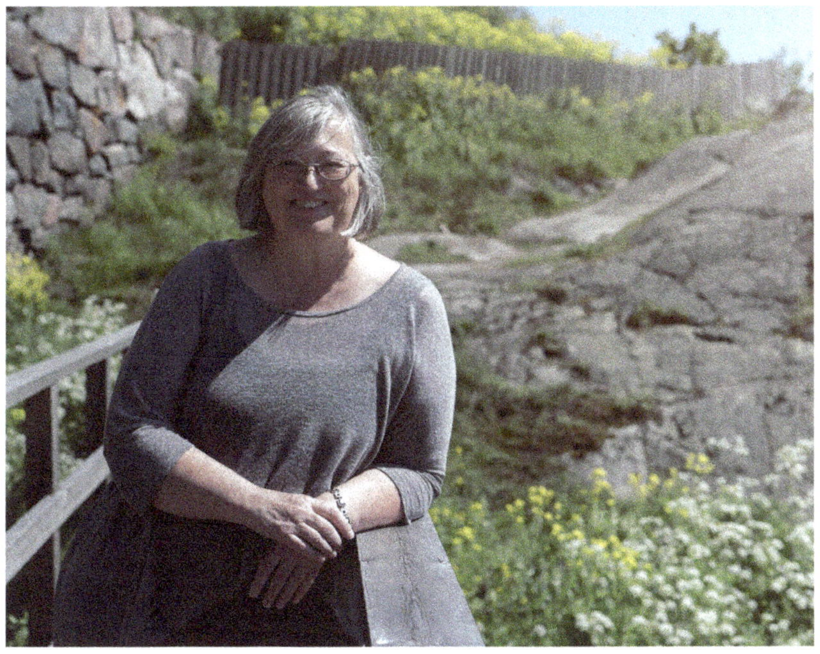

Tracey Warr. Photo by Sergio Urbina.

Tracey Warr is a fiction and non-fiction writer based in France. She describes herself as writing in the vicinity of art. She is an avid swimmer.

Tracey Warr's historical novels, set in France, England and Wales, are published by Meanda Books: *Almodis the Peaceweaver* (2011), *The Viking Hostage* (2014), *Conquest I: Daughter of the Last King* (2016), *Conquest II: The Drowned Court* (2017) and *Conquest III: The Anarchy* (2020). Her fiction has received awards from Literature Wales and Santander and was shortlisted for the Impress Prize.

Her published work on contemporary art includes *The Artist's Body* (Phaidon, 2000), *Remote Performances in Nature and Architecture* (Routledge, 2015) and *The Midden* (Garret, 2018). She has published numerous essays on contemporary artists with publishers including Intellect, Tate, Merrell/Barbican, Black Dog and Manchester University Press. She was an invited artist in the *Exoplanet Lot* exhibition and the *Frontiers in Retreat* five-year art and ecology research project.

She is working on a biography entitled *Three Female Lords,* about three sisters who lived in southern France and northern Spain in the 11th century. The biography has been supported by an Authors' Foundation Award.

She was Head of Dartington Arts School and established MA Poetics of Imagination there with Martin Shaw. She was Senior Lecturer in art history and theory at Oxford Brookes University and Dartington College of Arts in the UK. She was Guest Professor at Bauhaus University, Weimar, Germany; MIT, Cambridge, US; and

Piet Zwart Institute, Rotterdam, Netherlands. She was Course Leader in Art History at Saint Francis University Study Abroad Programme in France. She has led many creative writing and art writing courses and workshops.

https://meandabooks.com
https://traceywarrwriting.com
www.facebook.com/traceywarrARTwriting
www.facebook.com/traceywarrhistoricalwriting
@TraceyWarr1